# POEMS
## 1965–1968

# Robert Graves

# POEMS 1965-1968

Doubleday & Company, Inc.
Garden City, New York
1969

# FOREWORD

These four groups of poems are additions to my *Collected Poems* 1965 (Cassell). XIX and XX have appeared in limited editions published in 1966 and 1967 by Messrs. Bertram Rota.

The contents of XXI and XXII are, with a few exceptions, more recent.

*Deyá*                                                    R.G
*Majorca*

# CONTENTS

## XIX

## XX

# XXI

# XXII

XIX

# COCK IN PULLET'S FEATHERS

Though ready enough with beak and spurs,
You go disguised, a cock in pullet's feathers,
Among those crowing, preening chanticleers.
But, dear self, learn to love your own body
In its full naked glory,
Despite all blemishes of moles and scars—
As she, for whom it shines, wholly loves hers.

# DEAD HAND

Grieve for the loveless, spiritless, faceless men
Without alternative but to protract
Reason's mortmain on what their hearts deny—
Themselves—and owed small courtesy beyond
The uncovered head, as when a hearse goes by.

# ARREARS OF MOONLIGHT

My heart lies wrapped in red under your pillow,
My body wanders banished among the stars;
On one terrestrial pretext or another
You still withhold the extravagant arrears
Of moonlight that you owe us,
Though the owl whoops from a far olive branch
His brief, monotonous, night-long reminder.

# WHAT DID YOU SAY?

She listened to his voice urgently pleading,
So captivated by his eloquence
She saw each word in its own grace and beauty
Drift like a flower down that clear-flowing brook,
And draw a wake of multicoloured bubbles.
But when he paused, intent on her reply,
She could stammer only: 'Love, what did you say?'—
As loath as ever to hold him in her arms
Naked, under the trees, until high day.

# LURE OF MURDER

A round moon suffocates the neighbouring stars
With greener light than sun through vine-leaves.
Awed by her ecstasy of solitude
I crouch among rocks, scanning the gulf, agape,
Whetting a knife on my horny sole.

Alas for the lure of murder, dear my love!
Could its employment purge two moon-vexed hearts
Of jealousy more formidable than death,
Then each would stab, stab, stab at secret parts
Of the other's beloved body where unknown
Zones of desire imperil full possession.

But never can mortal dagger serve to geld
This glory of ours, this loving beyond reason—
Death holds no remedy or alternative:
We are singled out to endure his lasting grudge
On the tall battlements of nightfall.

# THE GORGE

Yonder beyond all hopes of access
Begins your queendom; here is my frontier.
Between us howl phantoms of the long dead,
But the bridge that I cross, concealed from view
Even in sunlight, and the gorge bottomless,
Swings and echoes under my strong tread
Because I have need of you.

# ECSTASY OF CHAOS

When the immense drugged universe explodes
In a cascade of unendurable colour
And leaves us gasping naked,
This is no more than ecstasy of chaos:
Hold fast, with both hands, to that royal love
Which alone, as we know certainly, restores
Fragmentation into true being.

# STOLEN JEWEL

You weep whole heartedly—your shining tears
Roll down for sorrow, not like mine for joy.
Dear love, should we not scorn to treat each other
With palliatives and with placebos?

Under a blinding moon you took from me
This jewel of wonder, but unaware
That it was yielded only on condition
Of whole possession; that it still denies you
Strength or desire for its restitution.

What do you fear? My hand around your throat?
What do I fear? Your dagger through my heart?
Must we not rage alone together
In lofts of singular high starriness?

# THE SNAPPED THREAD

Desire, first, by a natural miracle
United bodies, united hearts, blazed beauty;
Transcended bodies, transcended hearts.

Two souls, now unalterably one
In whole love always and for ever,
Soar out of twilight, through upper air,
Let fall their sensuous burden.

Is it kind, though, is it honest even,
To consort with none but spirits—
Leaving true-wedded hearts like ours
In enforced night-long separation,
Each to its random bodily inclination,
The thread of miracle snapped?

# FORTUNATE CHILD

For fear strangers might intrude upon us
You and I played at being strangers,
But lent our act such verisimilitude
That when at last, by hazard, we met alone
In a secret glen where the badger earths
We had drawn away from love: did not prepare
For melting of eyes into hearts of flowers,
For a sun-aureoled enhancement of hair,
For over-riding of death on an eagle's back—
Yet so it was: sky shuddered apart before us
Until, from a cleft of more than light, we both
Overheard the laugh of a fortunate child
Swung from those eagle talons in a gold cloth.

# LOVING TRUE, FLYING BLIND

How often have I said before
That no soft 'if', no 'either-or',
Can keep my obdurate male mind
From loving true and flying blind?—

Which, though deranged beyond all cure
Of temporal reason, knows for sure
That timeless magic first began
When woman bared her soul to man.

Be bird, be blossom, comet, star,
Be paradisal gates ajar,
But still, as woman, bear you must
With who alone endures your trust.

# THE NEAR ECLIPSE

Out shines again the glorious round sun—
After his near-eclipse when pools of light
Thrown on the turf between leaf shadows
Grew crescent-shaped like moons—dizzying us
With paraboles of colour: regal amends
To our own sun mauled barbarously
By the same wide-mouthed dragon.

# DANCING FLAME

Pass now in metaphor beyond birds,
Their seasonal nesting and migration,
Their airy gambols, their repetitive song;
Beyond the puma and the ocelot
That spring in air and follow us with their eyes;
Beyond all creatures but our own selves,
Eternal genii of dancing flame
Armed with the irreproachable secret
Of love, which is: never to turn back.

# BIRTH OF ANGELS

Never was so profound a shadow thrown
On earth as by your sun: a black roundel
Harbouring an unheard-of generation
Fledged by the sun ablaze above your own—
Wild beyond words, yet each of them an angel.

## ON GIVING

Those who dare give nothing
Are left with less than nothing;
Dear heart, you give me everything,
Which leaves you more than everything—
Though those who dare give nothing
Might judge it left you nothing.

Giving you everything,
I too, who once had nothing,
Am left with more than everything
As gifts for those with nothing
Who need, if not our everything,
At least a loving something.

17

# THE P'ENG THAT WAS A K'UN

*(Adapted from the Chinese of Lao Tse)*

In Northern seas there roams a fish called K'un,
Of how many thousand leagues in length I know not,
Which changes to a bird called P'eng—its wing-span
Of how many thousand leagues in width I know not.
Every half-year this P'eng, that was a K'un,
Fans out its glorious feathers to the whirlwind
And soars to the most Southerly pool of Heaven.

The Finch and Sparrow, thus informed, debated:
'We by our utmost efforts may fly only
To yonder elm. How can the P'eng outdo us?
Though, indeed, neither started as a fish.'

# LIKE OWLS

The blind are their own brothers; we
Form an obscure fraternity
Who, though not destitute of sight
Know ourselves doomed from birth to see,
Like owls, most clearly in half light.

# IN PERSPECTIVE

What, keep love in *perspective?*—that old lie
Forced on the Imagination by the Eye
Which, mechanistically controlled, will tell
How rarely table-sides run parallel;
How distance shortens us; how wheels are found
Oval in shape far oftener than round;
How every ceiling-corner's out of joint;
How the broad highway tapers to a point—
Can all this fool us lovers? Not for long:
Even the blind will sense that something's wrong.

# THE UTTER RIM

But if that Cerberus, my mind, should be
Flung to earth by the very opiate
That frees my senses for undared adventure,
Waving them wide-eyed past me to explore
Limitless hells of disintegrity,
Endless, undifferentiatable fate
Scrolled out beyond the utter rim of nowhere,
Scrolled out . . . . . .
               who on return fail to surrender
Their memory trophies, random wisps of horror
Trailed from my shins or tangled in my hair?

# UNICORN AND THE WHITE DOE

Unicorn with burning heart
Breath of love has drawn
On his desolate peak apart
At rumour of dawn,

Has trumpeted his pride
These long years mute,
Tossed his horn from side to side,
Lunged with his foot.

Like a storm of sand has run
Breaking his own boundaries,
Gone in hiding from the sun
Under camphor trees.

Straight was the course he took
Across the plain, but here with briar
And mire the tangled alleys crook,
Baulking desire.

A shoulder glistened white—
The bough still shakes—
A white doe darted out of sight
Through the forest brakes.

Tall and close the camphors grow
The grass grows thick—
Where you are I do not know,
You fly so quick.

Where have you fled from me?
I pursue, you fade,
I hunt, you hide from me
In the chequered glade.

Often from my hot lair
I would watch you drink,
A mirage of tremulous air,
At the pool's brink.

Vultures, rocking high in air
By the western gate,
Warned me with discordant cry
You are even such as I:
You have no mate.

(1920—recast 1966)

# BOWER-BIRD

The Bower-bird improvised a cool retreat
For the hen he honoured, doing his poor best
With parrot-plumage, orchids, bones and corals,
To engage her fancy.
                    But this was no nest . . .
So, though the Penguin dropped at his hen's feet
An oval stone to signal: 'be my bride',
And though the Jackdaw's nest was glorified
With diamond rings and brooches massed inside,
It was the Bower-bird who contented me
By not equating love with matrimony.

# MIST

Fire and Deluge, rival pretenders
To ruling the world's end; these cannot daunt us
Whom flames will never singe, nor floods drown,
While we stand guard against their murderous child
Mist, that slily catches at love's throat,
Shrouding the clear sun and clean waters
Of all green gardens everywhere—
The twitching mouths likewise and furtive eyes
Of those who speak us fair.

# THE WORD

The Word is unspoken
Between honest lovers:
They substitute a silence
Or wave at a wild flower,
Sighing inaudibly.

That it exists indeed
Will scarcely be disputed:
The wildest of conceptions
Can be reduced to speech—
Or so the Schoolmen teach.

You and I, thronged by angels,
Learned it in the same dream
Which startled us by moon-light,
And that we still revere it
Keeps our souls aflame.

'God' is a standing question
That still negates an answer.
The Word is not a question
But simple affirmation,
The antonym of 'God'.

Who would believe this Word
Could have so long been hidden
Behind a candid smile,
A sweet but hasty kiss
And always dancing feet?

# PERFECTIONISTS

Interalienation of their hearts
It was not, though both played resentful parts
In proud unwillingness to share
One house, one pillow, the same fare.
It was perfectionism, they confess,
To know the truth and ask for nothing less.

Their fire-eyed guardians watched from overhead:
'These two alone have learned to love,' they said,
'But neither can forget
They are not worthy of each other yet.'

# PRISON WALLS

Love, this is not the way
To treat a glorious day:
To cloud it over with conjectured fears,
Wiping my eyes before they brim with tears
And, long before we part,
Mourning the torments of my jealous heart.

That you have tried me more
Than who else did before,
Is no good reason to prognosticate
My last ordeal: when I must greet with hate
Your phantom fairy prince
Conjured in childhood, lost so often since.

Nor can a true heart rest
Resigned to second best—
Why did you need to temper me so true
That I became your sword of swords, if you
Must nail me on your wall
And choose a painted lath when the blows fall?

Because I stay heart-whole,
Because you bound your soul
To mine, with curses should it wander free,
I charge you now to keep full faith with me
Nor can I ask for less
Than your unswerving honest-heartedness.

Then grieve no more, but while
Your flowers are scented, smile
And never sacrifice, as others may,
So clear a dawn to dread of Judgement Day—
Lest prison walls should see
Fresh tears of longing you let fall for me.

# A DREAM OF HELL

You reject the rainbow
Of our Sun castle
As hyperbolic;

You enjoin the Moon
Of our pure trysts
To condone deceit;

Lured to violence
By a lying spirit,
You break our troth.

Seven wide, enchanted
Wards of horror
Lie stretched before you,

To brand your naked breast
With impious colours,
To band your thighs.

How can I discharge
Your confused spirit
From its chosen hell?

You who once dragged me
From the bubbling slime
Of a tidal reach,

Who washed me, fed me,
Laid me in white sheets,
Warmed me in brown arms,

Would you have me cede
Our single sovereignty
To your tall demon?

# OUR SELF

When first we came together
It was no chance foreshadowing
Of a chance happy ending.
The case grows always clearer
By its own worse disorder:
However reasonably we oppose
That unquiet integer, our self, we lose.

# BITES AND KISSES

Heather and holly,
Bites and kisses,
A courtship-royal
On the hill's red cusp.
Look up, look down,
Gaze all about you—
A livelier world
By ourselves contrived:

Swan in full course
Up the Milky Way,
Moon in her wildness,
Sun ascendant
In Crab or Lion,
Beyond the bay
A pride of dolphins
Curving and tumbling
With bites and kisses . . .

Or dog-rose petals
Well-starred by dew,
Or jewelled pebbles,
Or waterlilies open
For the dragon-flies
In their silver and blue.

## SUN-FACE AND MOON-FACE

We twin cherubs above the Mercy Seat,
Sun-face and Moon-face,
Locked in the irrevocable embrace
That guards our children from defeat,
Are fire not flesh; as none will dare deny
Lest his own soul should die.

# FREEHOLD

Though love expels the ugly past
Restoring you this house at last—
This generous-hearted mind and soul
Reserved from alien control—
How can you count on living free
From sudden jolts of history,
From interceptive sigh or stare
That heaves you back to how-things-were
And makes you answerable for
The casualties of bygone war?
Yet smile your vaguest: make it clear
That then was then, but now is here.

# THE NECKLACE

Variegated flowers, nuts, cockle-shells
And pebbles, chosen lovingly and strung
On golden spider-webs with a gold clasp
For your neck, naturally: and each bead touched
By a child's lips as he stoops over them:
Wear these for the new miracle they announce—
All four cross-quarter-days beseech you—
Your safe return from shipwreck, drought and war,
Beautiful as before, to what you are.

## A BRACELET

A bracelet invisible
For your busy wrist,
Twisted from silver
Spilt afar,
From silver of the clear Moon,
From her sheer halo,
From the male beauty
Of a shooting star.

# BLACKENING SKY

Lightning enclosed by a vast ring of mirrors,
Instant thunder extravagantly bandied
Between red cliffs no hawk may nest upon,
Triumphant jetting, passion of deluge: ours—
With spray that stuns, dams that lurch and are gone. . . .

But against this insensate hubbub of subsidence
Our voices, always true to a fireside tone,
Meditate on the secret marriage of flowers
Or the bees' paradise, with much else more;
And while the sky blackens anew for rain,
On why we love as none ever loved before.

# BLESSED SUN

Honest morning blesses the Sun's beauty;
Noon, his endurance; dusk, his majesty;
Sweetheart, our own twin worlds bask in the glory
And searching wisdom of that single eye—
Why must the Queen of Night on her moon throne
Tear up their contract and still reign alone?

# LION-GENTLE

Love, never disavow our vow
Nor wound your lion-gentle:
Take what you will, dote on it, keep it,
But pay your debts with a grave, wilful smile
Like a woman of the sword.

# SPITE OF MIRRORS

O what astonishment if you
Could see yourself as others do,
Foiling the mirror's wilful spite
That shows your left cheek as the right
And shifts your lovely crooked smile
To the wrong corner! But meanwhile
Lakes, pools and puddles all agree
(Bound in a vast conspiracy)
To reflect only your stern look
Designed for peering in a book—
No easy laugh, no glint of rage,
No thoughts in cheerful pilgrimage,
No start of guilt, no rising fear,
No premonition of a tear.

How, with a mirror, can you keep
Watch on your eyelids closed in sleep?
How judge which profile to bestow
On a new coin or cameo?
How, from two steps behind you, stare
At your firm nape discovered bare
Of ringlets as you bend and reach
Transparent pebbles from the beach?
Love, if you long for a surprise
Of self-discernment, hold my eyes
And plunge deep down in them to see
Sights never long withheld from me.

# PRIDE OF LOVE

I face impossible feats at your command,
Resentful at the tears of love you shed
For the faint-hearted sick who flock to you;
But since all love lies wholly in the giving,
Weep on: your tears are true,
Nor can despair provoke me to self-pity
Where pride alone is due.

# HOODED FLAME

Love, though I sorrow, I shall never grieve:
Grief is to mourn a flame extinguished;
Sorrow, to find it hooded for the hour
When planetary influences deceive
And hope, like wine, turns sour.

# INJURIES

Injure yourself, you injure me:
Is that not true as true can be?
Nor can you give me cause to doubt
It works the other way about;
So what precautions must I take
Not to be injured for love's sake?

# HER BRIEF WITHDRAWAL

'Forgive me, love, if I withdraw awhile:
It is only that you ask such bitter questions,
Always another beyond the extreme last.
And the answers astound: you have entangled me
In my own mystery. Grant me a respite:
I was happier far, not asking, nor much caring,
Choosing by appetite only: self-deposed,
Self-reinstated, no one observing.
When I belittled this vibrancy of touch
And the active vengeance of these folded arms
No one could certify my powers for me
Or my saining virtue, or know that I compressed
Knots of destiny in a careless fist,
I who had passed for a foundling from the hills
Of innocent and flower-like phantasies,
Though minting silver by my mere tread . . . .
Did I not dote on you, I well might strike you
For implicating me in your true dream.'

# THE CRANE

The Crane lounes loudly in his need,
    And so for love I loune:
Son to the sovereign Sun indeed,
    Courier of the Moon.

# STRANGENESS

You love me strangely, and in strangeness
I love you wholly, with no parallel
To this long miracle; for each example
Of love coincidence levels a finger
At strangeness undesigned as unforeseen.

And this long miracle is to discover
The inmost you and never leave her;
To show no curiosity for another;
To forge the soul and its desire together
Gently, openly and for ever.

Seated in silence, clothed in silence
And face to face—the room is small
But thronged with visitants—
We ask for nothing: we have all.

## SONG: HOW CAN I CARE?

How can I care whether you sigh for me
    While still I sleep alone swallowing back
The spittle of desire, unmanned, a tree
    Pollarded of its crown, a dusty sack
    Tossed on the stable rack?

How can I care what coloured frocks you wear,
    What humming-birds you watch on jungle hills,
What phosphorescence wavers in your hair,
    Or with what water-music the night fills—
    Dear love, how can I care?

# SONG: THOUGH ONCE TRUE LOVERS

Though once true lovers,
    We are less than friends.
What woman ever
    So ill-used her man?
That I played false
    Not even she pretends:
May God forgive her,
    For, alas, I can.

## SONG: CHERRIES OR LILIES

Death can have no alternative but Love,
Or Love but Death.
Acquaintance dallying on the path of Love,
Sickness on that of Death,
Pause at a bed-side, doing what they can
With fruit and flowers bought from the barrow man.

Death can have no alternative but Love,
Or Love but Death.
Then shower me cherries from your orchard, Love,
Or strew me lilies, Death:
For she and I were never of that breed
Who vacillate or trifle with true need.

# SONG: CROWN OF STARS

Lion-heart, you prowl alone
True to Virgin, Bride and Crone;
None so black of brow as they
Now, tomorrow, yesterday.
Yet the night you shall not see
Must illuminate all three
As the tears of love you shed
Blaze about their single head
And a sword shall pierce the side
Of true Virgin, Crone and Bride
Among mansions of the dead.

## SONG: THE PALM TREE

Palm-tree, single and apart
    In your serpent-haunted land,
Like the fountain of a heart
    Soaring into air from sand—
None can count it as a fault
That your roots are fed with salt.

Panniers-full of dates you yield,
    Thorny branches laced with light,
Wistful for no pasture-field
    Fed by torrents from a height,
Short of politics to share
With the damson or the pear.

Never-failing phoenix tree
    In your serpent-haunted land,
Fount of magic soaring free
    From a desert of salt sand;
Tears of joy are salty too—
Mine shall flow in praise of you.

## SONG: FIG TREE IN LEAF

One day in early Spring
Upon bare branches perching
    Great companies of birds are seen
    Clad all at once in pilgrim green
Their news of love to bring:

Their fig tree parable,
For which the world is watchful,
    Retold with shining wings displayed:
    Her secret flower, her milk, her shade,
Her scarlet, blue and purple.

# SONG: DEW-DROP AND DIAMOND

The difference between you and her
(Whom I to you did once prefer)
Is clear enough to settle:
She like a diamond shone, but you
Shine like an early drop of dew
Poised on a red rose-petal.

The dew-drop carries in its eye
Mountain and forest, sea and sky,
With every change of weather;
Contrariwise, a diamond splits
The prospect into idle bits
That none can piece together.

## *SONG:* SULLEN MOODS

Love, never count your labour lost
    Though I turn sullen or retired
Even at your side; my thought is crossed
    With fancies by no evil fired.

And when I answer you, some days,
    Vaguely and wildly, never fear
That my love walks forbidden ways,
    Snapping the ties that hold it here.

If I speak gruffly, this mood is
    Mere indignation at my own
Shortcomings, plagues, uncertainties:
    I forget the gentler tone.

You, now that you have come to be
    My one beginning, prime and end,
I count at last as wholly me,
    Lover no longer nor yet friend.

Help me to see you as before
    When overwhelmed and dead, almost,
I stumbled on that secret door
    Which saves the live man from the ghost.

Be once again the distant light,
    Promise of glory, not yet known
In full perfection—wasted quite
    When on my imperfection thrown.

## SONG: JUST FRIENDS

Just friend, you are my only friend—
You think the same of me
And swear our love must never end
Though lapped in secrecy,
As all true love should be.
They ask us: 'What about you two?'
I answer 'Only friends' and you:
'Just friends' gently agree.

## SONG: OF COURSE

No, of course we were never
    Off course in our love,
Being nourished by manna
    That dripped from above,

And our secret of loving
    Was taught us, it seems,
By ravens and owlets
    And fast-flowing streams.

We had sealed it with kisses,
    It blazed from our eyes,
Yet all was unspoken
    And proof against lies.

For to publish a secret
    Once learned in the rain
Would have meant to lose course
    And not find it again.

So this parting, of course,
    Is illusion, not fate,
And the love in your letters
    Comes charged overweight.

# *SONG:* THREE RINGS FOR HER

Flowers remind of jewels;
Jewels, of flowers;
Flowers, of innocent morning;
Jewels, of honest evening—
Emerald, moonstone, opal—
For so I mean, and meant.
Jewels are longer lasting—
Emerald, moonstone, opal;
Opal, emerald, moonstone:
Moonstone, opal, emerald—
And wear a livelier scent.

## SINCÈREMENT

J'étais confus à cet instant.
Quelle honte d'avoir écrit
L'adverbe aveugle 'sincèrement'—
'Je t'aime' m'aurait suffi
Sans point et sans souci.

## DANS UN SEUL LIT

Entre deux belles femmes dans un seul lit
Cet homme, se sentant interdit,
Des convenances n'ose pas faire foin
Mais opte pour elle qu'il aime le moins.

Entre deux beaux hommes en pareil cas,
Une dame sans moeurs si délicats
Mais sans s'exprimer en termes crus,
Se penche vers lui qu'elle aime le plus.

# POSSIBLY

*Possibly* is not a monosyllable;
    Then answer me
At once if possible
    Monosyllabically,
*No* will be good, *Yes* even better
Though longer by one letter.

*Possibly* is not a monosyllable,
    And my heart flies shut
At the warning rumble
    Of a suspended *But* . . .
O love, be brief and exact
In confession of simple fact.

# IS NOW THE TIME?

If he asks, 'Is now the time?', it is not the time.
She turns her head from his concern with time
As a signal not to haste it;
And every time he asks: 'Is now the time?'
A hundred nights are wasted.

# TWINS

Siamese twins: one, maddened by
The other's moral bigotry,
Resolved at length to misbehave
And drink them both into the grave.

# SAIL AND OAR

Woman sails, man must row:
Each, disdainful of a tow,
Cuts across the other's bows
Shame or fury to arouse—
And evermore it shall be so,
Lest man sail, or woman row.

# GOOSEFLESH ABBEY

Nuns are allowed fully liberty of conscience.
Yet might this young witch, when she took the veil,
Count on an aged Abbess's connivance
At keeping toad-familiars in her cell?
Some called it liberty; but others, licence—
And how was she to tell?

# THE HOME-COMING

At the tangled heart of a wood I fell asleep,
Bewildered by her silence and her absence—
As though such potent lulls in love were not
Ordained by the demands of pure music.

A bird sang: 'Close your eyes, it is not for long—
Dream of what gold and crimson she will wear
In honour of your oak-brown.'

It was her hoopoe. Yet, when the spread heavens
Of my feast night glistened with shooting stars
And she walked unheralded up through the dim light
Of the home lane, I did not recognise her—
So lost a man can be
Who feeds on hopes and fears and memory.

# WITH THE GIFT OF A LION'S CLAW

Queen of the Crabs, accept this claw
Plucked from a Lion's patient paw;
It shall propel her forward who
Ran sideways always hitherto.

# WIGS AND BEARDS

In the bad old days a bewigged country Squire
Would never pay his debts, unless at cards,
Shot, angled, urged his pack through standing grain,
Horsewhipped his tenantry, snorted at the arts,
Toped himself under the table every night,
Blasphemed God with a cropful of God-damns,
Aired whorehouse French or lame Italian,
Set fashions of pluperfect slovenliness
And claimed seigneurial rights over all women
Who slept, imprudently, under the same roof.

Taxes and wars long ago ploughed them under—
'And serve the bastards right' the Beards agree,
Hurling their empties through the café window
And belching loud as they proceed downstairs.
Latter-day bastards of that famous stock,
They never rode a nag, nor gaffed a trout,
Nor winged a pheasant, nor went soldiering,
But remain true to the same hell-fire code
In all available particulars
And scorn to pay their debts even at cards.
Moreunder (which is to subtract, not add),
Their ancestors called themselves gentlemen
As they, in the same sense, call themselves artists.

## PERSONAL PACKAGING, INC.

Folks, we have zero'd in to a big break-thru:
Our boys are learning how to package *people*
By a new impermeable-grading process
In cartons of mixed twenties—all three sexes!

Process involves molecular adjustment
To micro-regulated temperatures,
Making them unexpendable time-wise
Thru a whole century . . . Some clients opt for
Five thousand years, or six, in real deep freeze—
A chance what sensible guy would kick against
To pile up dollars at compound interest?
Nor do we even propose that they quit smoking
Or, necessarily, be parted from their wives.

# WORK ROOM

Camp-stool for chair once more and packing case for table;
All histories of doubt extruded from this room
With its menacing, promising, delusive, toppling bookshelves;
Nothing now astir but you in my fresh imagination,
And no letters but yours ever demanding answers.
To start all over again; indeed, why should I not?—
With a new pen, clean paper, full inkpot.

# THE ARK

Beasts of the field, fowls likewise of the air,
Came trooping, seven by seven or pair by pair;
And though from Hell the arch-fiend Samael
Bawled out 'Escapist!' Noah did not care.

# ALL EXCEPT HANNIBAL

Trapped in a dismal marsh, he told his troops:
'No lying down, lads! Form your own mess-groups
And sit in circles, each man on the knees
Of the man behind; then nobody will freeze.'

They obeyed his orders, as the cold sun set,
Drowsing all night in one another's debt,
All except Hannibal himself, who chose
His private tree-stump—he was one of those!

# THE BEGGAR MAID AND KING COPHETUA

To be adored by a proud Paladin
Whom the wide world adored,
To queen it over countless noblewomen:
What fame was hers at last,
What lure and envy!

Yet, being still a daughter of the mandrake
She sighed for more than fame;
Not all the gold with which Cophetua crowned her
Could check this beggar-maid's
Concupiscence.

Sworn to become proverbially known
As martyred by true love,
She took revenge on his victorious name
That blotted her own fame
For woman's magic.

True to her kind, she slipped away one dawn
With a poor stable lad,
Gaunt, spotted, drunken, scrawny, desperate,
Mean of intelligence
As bare of honour.

So pitiable indeed that when the guards
Who caught them saw the green
Stain on her finger from his plain brass ring
They gaped at it, too moved
Not to applaud her.

# FOR EVER

Sweetheart, I beg you to renew and seal
With a not supererogatory kiss
Our contract of 'For Ever'.
                              Learned judges
Deplore the household sense 'interminable':
True love, they rule, never acknowledges
Future or past, only a perfect now. . . .
But let it read 'For Ever', anyhow!

## JUGUM IMPROBUM

Pyrrha, jugo tandem vitulum junges-ne leoni?
Sit tibi dilectus, num stricto verbere debet
Compelli pavitans medium moriturus in ignem.

## DE ARTE POETICA

De minimis curat non Lex, utcumque poeta.

## SIT MIHI TERRA LEVIS

Ante mortem qui defletus
Solis lucem repperit
Ante Mortem perquietus,
Erato, domum redit.

XXII

# TOUSLED PILLOW

She appeared in Triad—Youth, Truth, Beauty—
Full face and profiles whispering together
All night at my bed-foot.
                              And when dawn came
At last, from a tousled pillow resolutely
I made my full surrender:
'So be it, Goddess, claim me without shame
And tent me in your hair.'
                              Since when she holds me
As close as candlewick to candleflame
And from all hazards free,
My soul drawn back to its virginity.

# TO BE IN LOVE

To spring impetuously in air and remain
Treading on air for three heart-beats or four,
Then to descend at leisure; or else to scale
The forward-tilted crag with no hand-holds;
Or, disembodied, to carry roses home
From a Queen's garden—this is being in love,
Graced with *agilitas* and *subtilitas*
At which few famous lovers ever guessed
Though children may foreknow it, deep in dream,
And ghosts may mourn it, haunting their own tombs,
And peacocks cry it, in default of speech.

# FACT OF THE ACT

On the other side of the world's narrow lane
You lie in bed, your young breasts tingling
With imagined kisses, your lips puckered,
Your fists tight.

Dreaming yourself naked in my arms,
Free from discovery, under some holm oak;
The high sun peering through thick branches,
All winds mute.

Endlessly you prolong the moment
Of your delirium: a first engagement,
Silent, inevitable, fearful,
Honey-sweet.

Will it be so in fact? Will fact mirror
Your virginal ecstasies:
True love, uncircumstantial,
No blame, no shame?

It is for you, now, to say 'come';
It is for you, now, to prepare the bed;
It is for you as the sole hostess
Of your white dreams—

It is for you to open the locked gate,
It is for you to shake red apples down,
It is for you to halve them with your hands
That both may eat.

Yet expectation lies as far from fact
As fact's own after-glow in memory;
Fact is a dark return to man's beginnings,
Test of our hardihood, test of a wilful
And blind acceptance of each other
As also flesh.

## TO OGMIAN HERCULES

Your Labours are performed, your Bye-works too;
Your ashes gently drift from Oeta's peak.
Here is escape then, Hercules, from empire.

Lithe Hebë, youngest of all Goddesses,
Who circles on the Moon's broad threshing floor
Harboured no jealousy for Megara,
Augë, Hippolytë, Deianeira,
But grieved for each in turn. You broke all hearts,
Burning too Sun-like for a Grecian bride.

Rest your immortal head on Hebë's lap,
What wars you started let your sons conclude,
Meditate a new Alphabet, heal wounds,
Draw poets to you with long golden chains
But still go armed with club and lion's pelt.

# ARROW SHOTS

Only a madman could mistake,
    When shot at from behind a tree,
The whizz and thud that arrows make—
    Yours, for example, fired at me.

Some bows are drawn to blind or maim,
    I have known others drawn to kill,
But truth in love is your sole aim
    And proves your vulnerary skill.

Though often, drowsing at mid-day,
    I wince to find myself your mark,
Let me concede the hit, but say:
    'Your hand is steadiest after dark.'

# SHE TO HIM

To have it, sweetheart, is to know you have it
Rather than think you have it;
To think you have it is a wish to take it,
Though afterwards you would not have it—
And thus a fear to take it.
Yet if you know you have it, you may take it
And know that still you have it.

# WITHIN REASON

You have wandered widely through your own mind
And your own perfect body;
Thus learning, within reason, gentle one,
Everything that can prove worth the knowing.

A concise wisdom never attained by those
Bodiless nobodies
Who travel pen in hand through others' minds,
But without reason,
Feeding on manifold contradiction.

To stand perplexed by love's inconsequences
Like fire-flies in your hair
Or distant flashes of a summer storm:
Such are the stabs of joy you deal me
Who also wander widely through my mind
And still imperfect body.

# THE YET UNSAYABLE

It was always fiercer, brighter, gentler than could be told
Even in words quickened by Truth's dark eye:
Its absence, whirlpool; its presence, deluge;
Its time, astonishment; its magnitude,
A murderous dagger-point.
                                        So we surrender
Our voices to the dried and scurrying leaves
And choose our own long-predetermined path
From the unsaid to the yet unsayable
In silence of love and love's temerity.

# NONE THE WISER

They would be none the wiser, even could they overhear
My slurred ecstatic mumbling or grow somehow aware
Of eyes ablaze behind shut lids in the attic gloom.

Even if they adjured me on pain of death to disclose
All that I see and am when I so absent myself,
What would they make of steady, somnolent light-rings
Converging, violet-blue or green hypnotic gold,
Upon a warded peep-hole, as it were a rift in Space,
Through which I peer, as it might be into your eyes,
And pass disembodied, a spiral wisp or whorl
Tall, slanted, russet-red, crowned with a lunar nimbus?—
To you the central flow, the glow, the ease, the hush
Of music drawn through irrecoverable modes.
And then such after-glory, meteors across the heart
When I awake, astonished, in the bed where once you dreamed.

'Metaphysical', they would comment lamely, 'metaphysical';
But you would smile at me for leaving so much out.

# THE NARROW SEA

With you for mast and sail and flag,
And anchor never known to drag,
Death's narrow but oppressive sea
Looks not unnavigable to me.

# THE OLIVE-YARD

Now by a sudden shift of eye
The hitherto exemplary world
Takes on immediate wildness
And birds, trees, winds, the very letters
Of our childhood's alphabet, alter
Into rainbowed mysteries.

Flesh is no longer flesh, but power;
Numbers, no longer arithmetical,
Dance like lambs, fly like doves;
And silence falls at last, though silken branches
Gently heave in the near olive-yard
And vague cloud labours on.

Whose was the stroke of summer genius
Flung from a mountain fastness
Where the griffon-vulture soars
That let us read our shrouded future
As easily as a book of prayer
Spread open on the knee?